Jack Wing

The Great Chicago Lake Tunnel

The Causes Which Led to Its Conception; the Great Undertaking; etc.

Jack Wing

The Great Chicago Lake Tunnel
The Causes Which Led to Its Conception; the Great Undertaking; etc.

ISBN/EAN: 9783743403710

Manufactured in Europe, USA, Canada, Australia, Japa

Cover: Foto ©ninafisch / pixelio.de

Manufactured and distributed by brebook publishing software
(www.brebook.com)

Jack Wing

The Great Chicago Lake Tunnel

CHICAGO LAKE TUNNEL

THE

CAUSES WHICH LED TO ITS CONCEPTION; THE G
UNDERTAKING; OBSTACLES ENCOUNTERED;
HOW THE WORK WAS PERFORMED;
LAUNCH OF THE CRIB, ETC.

TOGETHER WITH

SKETCHES OF THE VISITS OF SEVERAL ILLUST
PARTIES TO THE WORKS, AND A MIDNIGHT
TRAIN OF CARS BENEATH LAKE
MICHIGAN.

ALSO, THE

SUCCESSFUL COMPLETION OF THE GREAT ENTERPRI

SPECIAL EDITION—ILLUSTRATED.

CHICAGO:
PUBLISHED BY JACK WING.
1867.

THE GREAT

CHICAGO LAKE TUNNEL.

THE

CAUSES WHICH LED TO ITS CONCEPTION; THE GREAT
UNDERTAKING; OBSTACLES ENCOUNTERED;
HOW THE WORK WAS PERFORMED;
LAUNCH OF THE CRIB, ETC.

TOGETHER WITH

SKETCHES OF THE VISITS OF SEVERAL ILLUSTRIOUS
PARTIES TO THE WORKS, AND A MIDNIGHT
TRAIN OF CARS BENEATH LAKE
MICHIGAN.

ALSO, THE

SUCCESSFUL COMPLETION OF THE GREAT ENTERPRISE.

_____

SPECIAL EDITION — ILLUSTRATED.

_____

CHICAGO:
PUBLISHED BY JACK WING.
1867.

THE GREAT
CHICAGO LAKE TUNNEL.

Ground was first broken for the great CHICAGO LAKE TUNNEL, on St. Patrick's Day, March 17th, 1864. The various causes which led to the undertaking of this gigantic work, and compelled such an enormous expenditure on the part of the city, may be briefly stated. The inhabitants of Chicago are painfully aware of them.

Since Chicago became a city, its great want had been an abundant supply of pure water. This want became more and more pressing as the city increased from a mere handful of settlers to be the teeming mart of the western world. Unlike most other cities, and especially those of the East, the surroundings of the Garden City were no more elevated than the place where the city itself stood, and no flow of water could be secured from any direction whatever. Indeed, the Chicago river possessed no current, being in fact a bayou setting back from the lake, its source on a precise dead level with its mouth.

The astonishing growth of the city, unparalleled in the history of the world, its increasing commerce and trade, combined to render the currentless river a cesspool of filth. Miles of sewerage were constructed, which discharged their foul contents into its turbid waters. Hundreds of steam tugs and lake craft plowed its surface, and the refuse and offal from numberless slaughter houses and packing establishments in the vicinity of Bridgeport, on the south branch, found its way into the filthy river. In midsummer, the stench emitted from this repository of a city's offal became intolerable; its waters grew thick and slimy, obliging the steam craft that plowed its surface to go far out into the lake to fill their boilers with pure water. Many terrible explosions have been yearly chronicled by the Chicago press, which resulted from the use of the foul water of the river for making steam. The animal matter which it contained generated gas, and explosions followed, which were often disastrous in the extreme.

The waters of Lake Michigan were contaminated and befouled by the influx, rather than current of the river, for a great distance from the shore. A short distance north of the mouth of the river, the engines of the city Water Works were at work, pumping this foul liquid into the reservoirs, from whence it found its way into every family in the city. Bridget had no other with which to fill her teakettle, and the laborer must needs quench his thirst with it. It came on the dinner table, and made the goblets look dirty; it was tasted from necessity, and that was all. The guests present, from cities blessed with pure water, disdained to taste it, and returned to their homes, declaring that they would not live in Chicago for the world, its water was "so filthy and smelt so bad."

Another grievous evil of the old water system was, that as cold weather approached, millions of infinitesimal fishes sought the enclosure near shore, from which the water was pumped. In spite of every effort, these scaly minnows would enter the reservoirs of the city, and come out in scores from every hydrant, alive and swimming. This was the greatest annoyance of all, and one that could not be brooked. Every drop of water drank in the city was highly flavored of fish, and one was obliged to look twice in his goblet to see that he did not swallow one alive.

This had been the precise condition of Chicago since it arose from the prairie to be the largest city in the western world. It was blessed with commerce; with unequaled resources and avenues of wealth; with railroads running to it from every quarter of the country, draining the bountifully yielding prairies, and pouring their products into its granaries and storehouses. Emigration flowed towards it with unchecked tide. Its people grew rich, its schools numerous; its magnificent churches could be counted by scores; its fine public buildings and private residences astonished the world. Its population increased to more than 250,000 souls. And Chicago was great, prosperous and happy, with the sole exception that it lacked the one great essential to vitality, to life itself and the life of its citizens, —PURE WATER.

AGITATION OF THE WATER QUESTION.

This state of things was endured quite submissively until the year 1863, when the citizens began to show a determination to have it ameliorated in some manner or another. The war was in progress, and the nation was too much excited for anybody to think of much else. Engineers, men of mind and ability all over the country, were turning their attention to the field. The pencil of the draughtsman was busy in outlining fortifications, bridging rivers and outwitting the rebel foe. The all-absorbing topic was the war. Men of wealth opened their purses and gave to the common cause; patriotic ladies and children did their best to help it to a triumph. The prospects were indeed poor for any great outlay in any other direction. But still the local agitation was kept up, until finally different parties began to submit plans and specifications for purifying the river.

Many of these devices were Yankee in the extreme, and not a few of them almost provoked a laugh. Perhaps the most elaborate of any was that prepared by Mr. Gindele, of the Board of Public Works. He suggested that the waters of the Calumet and Desplaines rivers be diverted into the Chicago river, by means of the feeder and the use of pumps. To this it was objected that the supply of water would be inadequate, while the adoption of the plan would involve the city in interminable and expensive chancery suits, the diversion of the current of the streams and of the canal seeming

8

necessarily to encroach upon rights which had vested in the canal company, and in the owners of mill property and water privileges on the canal and on the running streams.

A second plan suggested was, to build a series of intercepting sewers, similar in their nature to those which have lately been erected in the city of London, for the purification of the river Thames. These, it was thought by some, could be constructed along the margin of the river, as reservoirs for the filth passing within its borders and from the sewers, the contents thus received being emptied into the lake, or distributed over the country for purposes of agriculture. This suggestion had a theoretical value. The largest city of the world adopted it, at an enormous expense, but to the time of its consideration here, no results had been deduced which would warrant a certainty of probable success. The expenditure of money would be very great, and the loss of time would be considerable, and on so great an experiment, which had not in itself a fair prospect of success, our people were unwilling to enter.

A covered aqueduct was also proposed. This it was thought should be of the diameter of ten feet, to extend from the lake to the river, which it should enter at some point on the south side, a point at about Sixteenth street being designated. To this plan it was objected, that the obnoxious matter being emptied into the lake so near the point whence the lake water would be drawn, it would be corrupted and increase rather than diminish the evil complained of.

About this time the ship canal bill was killed, a result feared by many of our citizens. It deprived them of all hope of relief in this direction, and gave an impetus to the Tunnel project, which shortly afterwards gained great favor among all classes. Every scheme as yet presented had proved untenable, and the desired end—that of providing an abundance of pure water for Chicago—was quite as far off as ever. Only one point had been gained, and that was, the people had now become thoroughly aroused on the subject. The grand result shows what popular will and determination can accomplish.

A TUNNEL UNDER LAKE MICHIGAN.

The inventive genius of our citizens, and particularly of the different members of the Board of Public Works, was now thoroughly aroused. Western determination was at work, and Teutonic pluck was resolved to unloose the bull-dog's grip. We had plenty of pure water constantly in our view, tantalizing as the fact may appear. It was true that lake Michigan was quite as foul as the river, near its mouth, but at a certain distance from shore the water became as pure as Croton, cold and clear as crystal. The contaminating influences of the Chicago river possessed no power over the waters of the lake, at a distance of two miles from shore. Here, then, was an eternal reservoir, from which Chicago could derive pure water in abundance, long after the masonry of the Croton aqueducts should crumble. It was a glorious idea in embryo. How could this natural supply of water be appropriated and made to flow through the miles of pipes and numberless hydrants of the city? The water, to insure its constant purity, must be drawn from the lake, at a distance of at least two miles from shore, far beyond the murky influx of the river and the city sewers. It was a great problem, worthy of the mind of genius. And it was solved. Chicago possessed a mind and a man equal to the gigantic task.

To Mr. E. S. Chesbrough, the skillful and acomplished city engineer, belongs the credit of the original idea of constructing a tunnel, two miles in length, beneath the bed of lake Michigan, which should literally tap the lake from the bottom, at that distance from shore, and through which pure water should be conveyed into the reservoirs of the city. No sooner had Mr. Chesbrough conceived the idea of a tunnel, than he proceeded to investigate the subject.

He soon determined, in his own mind at least, that it was entirely feasible, and prepared plans for its construction, into which the other members of the Board of Public Works entered with a will.

On the 13th day of February, 1863, the amended city charter was approved, in which power was given to the city "to construct such aqueducts along the shore of lake Michigan, or in the highways, or elsewhere in said Cook county, and to construct such pumping works, breakwaters, subsiding basins, filter beds and reservoirs, and to lay such water mains, and to make all other constructions in said county, as shall be necessary in obtaining from lake Michigan a sufficient and abundant supply of pure water for said city;" "to extend aqueducts, or inlet pipes, into lake Michigan, so far as may be deemed necessary to insure a supply of pure water, and to erect a pier or piers in the navigable waters of said lake, for the making, preserving and working of said pipes or aqueducts."

Congress sanctioned this action of the Illinois State Legislature, January 16, 1864.

And so the Chicago Lake Tunnel became a tangible thing.

EXAMINATION OF THE BED OF LAKE MICHIGAN.

Soon after the action of the State Legislature, but before its sanction by Congress, the bed of the lake was examined, with a view to test the feasibility of excavating the Tunnel. In the month of June, 1863, the City Engineer, with some scientific aid, commenced boring to ascertain the nature of the bottom. The experiments were made first at some twenty feet from the shore. At about two hundred feet from the shore, the water being a little over twenty feet deep, there was blue clay underlying a sandy covering. These experiments led to others. Two scows were towed into the lake and secured by anchors. From between these a two-inch gas pipe was lowered until it rested on the surface of

the earth, the top being two or three feet above the surface of the water. Down this tube an auger was passed, both being capable of being lengthened by screwing additional parts to each. At three-quarters of a mile from the shore, the water being twenty feet deep, there was found a four-inch covering of sand and thirty feet of blue clay. One and three-quarters miles out, the water being thirty-one feet deep, the same substratum was discovered. Two miles and a quarter due east of the Water Works, near the site of the crib as at present located, the water, being thirty feet deep, was clear and cool. The earth was penetrated to the depth of thirty feet. Here was found a covering of sand and soft mashy clay, with a clay becoming more hard and compact as it was sunk into. On June 16th, of the same year, the temperature of the water began to be tested. Its clearness was apparent, a small object being visible at a distance of eighteen feet, the water being thirty-six feet deep. On the surface, the thermometer showed, at three o'clock of the 16th day of June, sixty degrees, and at the bottom, fifty-one and a half degrees. These experiments continued to be carried on with the like result of exhibiting a clay substratum, the approach to the shore, however, showing a deeper alluvial deposit, composed mainly of sand.

AWARD OF THE TUNNEL CONTRACT.

The result of the above experiments was the adoption of Mr. Chesbrough's idea of building a tunnel under the lake, which they demonstrated to be entirely practicable to the minds of the engineers. The old methods of purifying the river, the compound sewers, ship canals, windmills, etc., were at once abandoned; and it is said that the Board of Public Works occasionally laugh at their own folly, in once entertaining such plans, now that the correct one has been found.

All visitors to the Great Lake Tunnel must not fail to call at 128 Washington Street, next to Chamber of Commerce, and take out an Accident Insurance Policy for one year.

The *Travelers' Insurance Company,* of Chicago, organized in April 1865, under a special act of the Legislature of Illinois, is one of the Companies that has sustained itself nobly in this branch of Insurance. It contains among its Stockholders many of the principal business men of Chicago and the West, is managed by careful and experienced underwriters, and is in every respect reliable and worthy the support and patronage of western men.

With all that has been done up to the present time in this direction, Accident Insurance is still in its infancy.

There is no reasonable doubt but what this kind of protective Insurance is rapidly becoming just as popular, and is considered just as legitimate as Fire Insurance.

This Company have lately attached a new feature to their already permanently established Accident business. They are now issuing Policies covering *Death from any Cause,* with weekly compensation in case of accidental injury.

This feature will commend itself to the attention of the public as being something new and popular in underwriting. Their rates are all Cash, as low as can be adopted with safety, and are within the reach of all.

This Company pays Dividends to its Policyholders in advance.

Agencies are established, where Policies may be obtained in the principal Cities and Towns throughout the West.

TRAVELERS
Insurance Company of Chicago.
LIFE AND ACCIDENT.
Cash Capital, - - - $100,000.00.

OFFICERS:

ORVILLE PAGE, President. CHARLES L. CURRIER, Vice President.
HENRY W. KING, Treasurer. JOHN W. CLAPP, Secretary.

Home Office, 128 Washington Street.

LIST OF STOCKHOLDERS.

John Tyrrell, *Firm Burley & Tyrrell.*
Henry W. King, " *King, Kellogg & Co.*
W. E. Doggett, " *Doggett, Bassett & Hills.*
H. A. Hurlbut, " *J. H. Reed & Co.*
E. Frankenthal, " *E. Frankenthal & Co.*
Jacob Friedman, *Tobacconist.*
Wm. McKindly, *V. Prs. Mer. F. & M. Ins. Co.*
Wm. E. Rollo, *Sec'y* " " "
J. L. Stark, Jr., *Attorney at Law.*
N. Jewett, *of J. M. Bradstreet's Com'l Ag.*
Schuyler S. Benjamin, *Pro. Adams House.*
Charles Hitchcock, *Attorney at Law.*
Julius H. Currier, *Sec. Ill. Gen. Fire Ins. Co.*
D. W. Page, *firm Culver, Page & Hoyne.*
Simon Florsheim, *Insurance Broker.*
H. N. Hibbard, *Attorney at Law.*
George P. Lee, *Treas. Chicago & N. W. R'y.*
David A. Gage, *Prop'r Sherman House.*
C. C. Waite, " " "

Chas. L. Currier, *Sec'y Am. Fire Ins. Co.*
Richard Somers, *Prop'r Richmond House.*
N. N. West, " " "
D. L. Wells, *R. R. Contract. & Br. Builder.*
Robert Hill, *Prop'r Matteson House.*
C. H. Cram, *with Doggett, Bassett & Hills.*
H. Z. Culver, *firm Culver, Page & Hoyne.*
W. F. Wentworth, *Cashier Briggs House.*
F. W. Burnham, " "
John B. Drake, *Prop'r Tremont House.*
John J. Peacre, *Prop'r Adams House.*
Orville Page, *Prest. Travelers Ins. Co.*
M. A. Hoyne, *firm Culver, Page & Hoyne.*
Allen Gibson, *Prest. Rock River Ins. Co.*
J. H. McVicker, *Prop'r McVicker's Theatre.*
R. N. Isham, M.D., *Prof. &c., Chi. Med. Col.*
D. Goodwin, Jr., *Gen. Ag't Nat. Life Ins. Co.*
John W. Clapp, *Sec'y Travelers Ins. Co.*
Chas. N. Conkey, *New York.*

But it was only through such inquiry and examination—research deep and long—that the proper plan was at last obtained.

The necessary drawings and specifications were now prepared, under the never-wearying eye of Mr. Chesbrough. Advertisements for bids for building the CHICAGO LAKE TUNNEL soon astonished the world, appearing. in all the Chicago papers, and, as we believe, the New York dailies. Several letters containing "sealed proposals" or bids were soon received, which were opened on the 9th of September, 1863, in the presence of the Board of Public Works and nearly all the several parties proposing.

The bids were seven in number, and ranged very wide of each other, as follows:

James Andrews, of Pittsburg, Pa................	$230,548
Dull & Gowan, of Harrisburg, Pa...............	315,139
Walker, Wood & Robinson, of New York.......	315,000
Williams, McBean, Brown & Nelson, of Chicago.	490,000
Henry Nash, of Chicago (per lineal foot)........	.40
D. L. De Golyer, of Chicago....................	620,000
William Baldwin, of New York................	1,056,000

The question will be asked, why this disparity of bids? It arose from the fact of a difference of opinion existing among the different parties offering the proposals, as to the character of the soil beneath the lake. Some of them claimed that they would meet with sand or gravel in the work of excavation, which would render it both difficult and dangerous; while others argued that the soil would be uniformly of clay and easily tunneled.

Messrs. Dull & Gowan, of Harrisburg, Pa., gentlemen well known in the engineering world, although not the lowest bidders, were the only parties who made an unqualified proposal, taking all risks of soil, etc., upon themselves, and consequently the contract was awarded to them.

On the 5th of October, the following month, the Common Council of Chicago granted all necessary authority for building the Tunnel, so far as they were concerned, and ordered that the requisite bonds be issued.

The contract for this gigantic work, pronounced by

DESCENDING THE SHORE SHAFT.

[SEE PAGE 16.]

engineers of both hemispheres to be the greatest the world ever saw, and beside of which the tunneling of the Thames was mere child's play, was signed and sealed on the 28th day of October, 1863. This paper, which bound the contractors to undertake and complete the greatest project ever entered upon by men, and the city of Chicago to pay them for the same, together with the penalties of failure by either party, bears the signatures of James J. Dull and James Gowan, the contractors, and J. G. Gindele, Frederick Letz, O. J. Rose, and F. C. Sherman, Commissioners of the Board of Public Works, and specifies the completion of the work "on or before the first day of November, A. D. 1865." As will be seen hereafter, the time fixed for the completion of the work proved to be far too early. It was destined to be the work of years.

GROUND BROKEN FOR THE TUNNEL.

A delay of about two months in the casting of the huge cylinders for the shore shaft of the Tunnel, at Pittsburg, Pennsylvania, postponed the inauguration ceremonies until the 17th of March, 1864, on which day the first shovelful of earth was removed. These ceremonies were of an interesting character, every man participating in them feeling aware of the great undertaking upon which they were entering, and the disgrace which a failure would bring both upon themselves and the city. The ceremonies were witnessed by about a hundred gentlemen, among whom were Mayor Sherman, Messrs. Letz and Rose, of the Board of Public Works, Mr. S. S. Hayes, the City Comptroller, Messrs. E. S. Chesbrough, U. P. Harris, and a majority of the members of the Common Council. The Mayor made a few remarks appropriate to the occasion, and then took the pick and broke the ground, amid the cheers of the

161 Lake St., Chicago.

NORTHWESTERN AGENCY CLOTHES WRINGERS!

Manufactured by the Bailey Washing and Wringing Machine Co.

CLASSIFICATION AND PRICE LIST.

Class No. 1, Wringers with Cog Wheels.

		Retail Prices.	SIZE OF ROLL. Length.	Diam.
No. 2.	NOVELTY	$ 9 00.	10 inches.	1⅝ inches.
" 3.	"	11 00.	11 "	2 "
" 2.	CHAMPION,	9 00.	10 "	1⅝ "
" 3.	"	11 00.	11 "	2 "
" 4.	BENCH MACHINE,	12 00.	11 "	2⅛ "
" 2.	" "	16 00.	8 "	3 "
" 1.	" "	18 00.	10 "	3 "
A No. 1.	" "	20 00.	10 "	3 "
No. 2.	SET TUBS,	15 00.	8 "	3 "
" 1.	" "	17 00.	10 "	3 "
" 4.	" "	12 00.	11 "	2⅛ "

CLASS No. 2, WITHOUT COG WHEELS.

No. 1.	NOVELTY,	$ 7 50.	10 inches.	1⅝ inches.
" 1.	CHAMPION,	7 50.	10 "	1⅝ "

UNIVERSAL CLOTHES WRINGER!

Manufactured by the Metropolitan Washing Machine Co.

		Retail Prices.	SIZE OF ROLL. Length.	Diam.
No. 1.	HOTEL WRINGER, COG WHEEL,	$12 00.	11 inches.	2¼ inches.
" 1½.	FAMILY " " "	10 00.	11 "	1⅞ "
" 2.	" " " "	8 50.	9¾ "	1⅞ "
" 2½.	" " without Cogs,	7 50.	10 "	1⅝ "
" 8.	LARGE HOTEL WRINGER, with Cogs,	18 00.	14 "	2⅛ "
" 18.	LAUNDRY, STEAM OR HAND,	30 00.	17¼ "	2¼ "
" 22.	LARGE LAUNDRY, "	45 00.	17½ "	3¼ "
" 2.	SHERMAN IRON FRAME,	8 00.	10 "	1⅞ "
" 2.	" " "	7 50.	10 "	1⅝ "
" 3.	NEW WORLD,	7 50.	10 "	1⅝ "

DOTY'S CLOTHES WASHER!

Family size,.......$14.00. Hotel size,.......$16.00.

Purrington's Patent Roll Carpet Sweeper!

☞CLOTHES WRINGERS REPAIRED.☜

JAS. R. RICE,
161 Lake St., Chicago.

company. Each of the gentlemen took a shovelful of earth
and placed it in the wheelbarrow, which was taken away by
Colonel Gowan, one of the contractors. The field was then
abandoned to Messrs. Dull & Gowan, and the work placed
in their hands; the Board reserving the right to examine
and criticise the operations as they progressed.

The location of the shore shaft was on the site of the old
pumping works, at the east end of Chicago avenue, directly
on the lake shore, about half an hour's walk from the Court
House.

SINKING OF THE SHORE SHAFT.

Messrs. Dull & Gowan, the contractors, now entered
zealously upon their great enterprise. A shaft about nine
feet in diameter was sunk, on the above site, a short distance
from the shore of the lake. When the workmen had
descended a short distance into the earth, they encountered
a bed of shifting quicksand, which for a time defied all efforts
at excavation. It was originally intended to construct the
shaft wholly of brick, running it down from the surface of
the ground, to a depth of fifteen feet below the level of the
bottom of the lake, but encountering the quicksand compelled the abandonment of this method. The contract was
consequently deviated from, and the contractors were author-
ized to run down an iron cylinder of the same dimensions as
the center of the crib, as far as the bottom of the sand bed,
about twenty-six feet. This inlet cylinder is nine feet in
diameter, inside, and two and a quarter inches thick. It is
cast in four sections of about nine feet in length. The great
labor of sinking these sections will be apparent to all.
From the bottom of the cylinders, twenty-six feet, the shaft
was continued into the earth until it reached the depth of
sixty-nine feet, being constructed of brick from the point
where the iron cylinders ceased.

This shaft is not unlike an immense well. It was destined to be the great highway through which the clay
excavated from the Tunnel proper should be conveyed to the

outer world, and much satisfaction was felt by the contractors when this bare commencement of their great work
was accomplished.

Over the mouth of this shaft, a rough, temporary building
was erected, large enough to contain a steam engine of great
power, the office of the contractors, and the brick, cement,
tools, etc., used by the workmen. An elevator was now
constructed, which carried the miners up and down the shaft
to their work, being propelled by the engine. Stepping
upon this platform, half a dozen hardy miners, carrying
each his little lamp, pick and shovel, would descend far
beneath the view of the spectators to their labors in the
bowels of the earth. The clay which they excavated was
brought up the shaft in the same manner, and the brick,
cement, etc., carried down.

At the bottom of the shaft water soon began to ooze in,
and it became necessary to construct a pump, which was
worked by the engine, and which kept it dry.

EXCAVATING THE TUNNEL PROPER.

At the depth of sixty-nine feet the workmen stopped, and
the shore "shaft" was pronounced a success. Here began
that nice engineering, which one of the editors of the London *Times*, who had visited the Tunnel, pronounced "the
greatest of modern times."

The point in the lake where the Tunnel should receive
water had already been fixed, by means of soundings, and
buoys marked the spot. An imaginary straight line was
drawn, which the Tunnel was to follow from the point where
it crossed the shaft, which was little less than prolonging a
straight line nine feet in length, without deviation, until it
reached some point two miles ahead. The compass, the
natural reliance of man upon the lake, could not be relied

upon *under* the lake. Local attractions of the earth would render it uselessly inaccurate, so far as giving anything more than a general direction was concerned. The only method of procedure was to run the axis of the Tunnel parallel with the straight line drawn over the lake, which was only observable at the point where it crossed the shaft.

With this, to less scientific minds than those engaged in the great work, frail reliance, the miners struck their picks into the hard clay at the bottom of the shaft, and excavating was commenced directly lakewards. The clay was thrown upon the elevator before mentioned, and drawn up the shaft, while an ingenious apparatus was arranged which carried it off and "dumped" it.

The width of the Tunnel, when bricked up, was decided to be five feet, and its clear height five feet two inches, the top and bottom arches being semi-circles. Two miners were all that could work upon the excavation ahead of the masons who laid the brick, and they were relieved at regular intervals, so that the work should not stop for a moment. The brick masonry, which followed the miners as fast as they advanced, was eight inches thick, the bricks being laid lengthwise of the Tunnel, with toothing joints, to give it greater strength and durability. Between this masonry and the sides of the excavation, as much of the earth was forced back as possible. The lower half of the bore was constructed in such a manner that the bricks lie against the clay, while in the upper half the bricks were wedged in between the brick and the earth, thus preventing any danger which might result from the tremendous pressure which it was feared might burst in the Tunnel.

The material used in the masonry was white Illinois brick, of the usual size, laid in cement. The Tunnel was to have a slope from the "crib," or lake terminus, to the shore, of two feet to the mile, to admit of its being emptied in case repairs should at any future time be necessary, the water being shut off by means of gates at the lake end.

In this slow and tedious manner, the workmen made their way under the lake, from fourteen to twenty feet being considered great progress for twenty-four hours, the work being continued night and day. Before they had advanced far from the shaft, the air began to grow impure, and each day the difficulty increased. Here was an obstacle of no small moment to encounter. A large steam bellows was obtained, and placed at the mouth of the shaft, from which piping, not unlike ordinary stove pipe, was run down the shaft, branching off into the Tunnel. This tube was perforated with holes, in such a manner that the operation of the bellows extracted the impure or dead air from the Tunnel, causing pure oxygen to fill its place, which in turn was carried off by the pipe, when it was consumed by the lungs of the workmen. As the Tunnel progressed, this pipe was lengthened, and thus a constant supply of pure air was obtained.

Soon it became necessary to provide some more rapid means of transporting the earth from the face of the excavation to the shaft. Rails were laid down, and small cars placed upon them. At the commencement these cars were propelled to the shaft by workmen, where they were drawn up, and their contents discharged. But as the distance increased, day by day, and new lengths of rail were added, other means of locomotion were sought. Much to the edification of the laborers, two small mules were purchased, which could barely stand between the walls of the Tunnel without rubbing their ears. After some little schooling, these tractable animals were placed upon the elevator, and lowered into the earth. After a little experience and training, they learned their work, and performed it well.

Several cars at a time were now loaded, and the mules attached, which drew them to the shaft. A regular railroad time-table was prepared, to avoid collisions, as it was impossible for any person entering the bore to pass the "down" train, should he be so unlucky as to encounter it in the bowels of the earth. At the shaft, the mules were turned around, and the train of empty cars drawn back. These mules and their long train of cars, presented a very pictur-

esque appearance, each of them wearing a small lamp upon his collar, which served for the calcium light before the engine.   This submarine railroading will be further spoken of in another chapter.

When the Tunnel had reached the distance of one thousand feet from the shaft, a sort of chamber or stopping place was made, where the excavation was enlarged, to afford a deposit for the material used, a place to mix the cement, turn-tables for the cars, stables for the mules, etc.   These were left at the distance of one thousand feet apart, to be bricked up when the whole work was completed.   The distance was marked upon the inside of the bore, as fast as the work progressed from the shaft, every five feet.

THE CRIB, AND ITS SUCCESSFUL LAUNCH.

The "crib," as it has been commonly called, was built on shore, and launched, much like the *Great Eastern* or any other sea-going hulk.   It is composed of huge timbers and tons of iron, no expense being spared to make it strong ; is forty feet and a half high and built in pentagonal form, in a circumscribed circle of ninety-eight and a half feet in diameter.   It was constructed with three walls—the outer, the center, and the inner—making it almost like three distinct structures, one inside the other, and all firmly braced and bolted together, so as to constitute one great structure.   Each of these walls was calked and tarred, like the hulk of a vessel.   They were constructed of twelve-inch square timber, the first twelve feet from the top of white oak and the remaining twenty-eight feet of white pine.   Each piece of timber comprising either wall was firmly bolted in its place with square rods of iron, one and five-sixteenths of an inch in diameter and thirty inches long.   The bottom was composed of twelve-inch timbers, held in place by bolts

thirty-six inches in length, passing through three distinct layers of timber. The whole framework was a combination of massive timbers and irons, firmly held together by bars and bolts and braced in every direction. When finished it contained fifteen separate watertight compartments. In the center was a "well," open at the bottom and top, through which the shaft was to descend into the bottom of the lake.

Each angle of the crib was provided with iron armor, to protect it from ice or any other body borne upon the waves. This covering was of iron two and a half inches thick, and covered the structure two feet each way from the angles, and extended downwards from the top twelve feet. This armor was fastened to the outer wall of the crib and the adjacent timbers by iron bolts thirty inches long, and to the inner wall and its timbers by round iron bolts, an inch and a half in diameter and thirteen and a half feet in length.

That people may form a correct idea of this immense structure, and the importance it possessed in the great work, we give a few items of the timber and iron used in its construction. It cost not far from one hundred thousand dollars before it was moved from the stocks. Reduced to board measure, there were used in building it 618,325 feet of lumber, as follows:

> 538,368 feet white pine timber.
> 42,000 " white oak timber.
> 20,000 " two-inch white pine plank.
> 18,000 " two-inch white oak plank.

Besides this, there were used five hundred bales of oakum and sixty-five tons of iron bolts.

This immense structure, almost as large as the Chicago Court House, was built like a vessel, on the north pier, a short distance from the mouth of the river. On the 24th day of July, 1865, an immense concourse of people gathered on the spot to see it launched. So great was the interest felt in its being successfully put in position, that merchants

Every Housekeeper should use it!

SILVER MEDAL AWARDED

TOURTELOT'S

EXTRACT ᴏꜰ BEEF

FOR MAKING A DELICIOUS

BEEF TEA OR SOUP.

This celebrated article should be in every household and in the possession of every traveler, as a most excellent soup or broth can be instantly prepared by the simple addition of boiling water.

It is put up in neat packages of one pound, and as it will not deteriorate by exposure to the air, can be used at any time after being opened, without fear of change.

FOR SALE BY DRUGGISTS AND GROCERS.

Price, $1.50 per Package.

Representing the Strength of 20 pounds of Fresh Beef.

TOURTELOT BROTHERS,

Preserved Meats, Game, Fish, Soups, etc.,

P. O. Box 2425.   *CHICAGO, ILL.*

Invaluable to Travelers and Invalids.

WORKING UPON THE "FACE" OF THE TUNNEL.

left their counting-rooms and hurried to the scene. Thousands of people were present, standing upon the house tops, riding upon the river in yawls, and seated in carriages upon the banks and piers.

The launch was announced to occur at between nine and ten o'clock in the morning. The day was propitious, scarcely a ripple breaking the surface of the lake. From the summit of the crib floated American flags, and the hat of Colonel Gowan was occasionally visible, as he went to and fro, giving orders to the workmen. The river itself presented a lively appearance. Seven tugboats, with flags flying and hundreds of people on their decks, among whom were Governor Oglesby, of Illinois, and many other distinguished men, were waiting in the harbor to tow the monster to its place in the lake.

Shortly after ten o'clock, the leviathan moved, rode slowly into the river, with streaming flags, and the hat of Colonel Gowan swinging over his head from the top. Cannon boomed, hundreds of steam whistles shrieked, bells rang, and thousands of throats cheered lustily. When about in the middle of the river, the mass left the ways upon which it rode, and rose upon the water as gracefully as any craft that ever was launched.

The tugboats now attached their hawsers, and the crib was towed slowly towards the buoys in the lake, which had been placed there to mark its position, on a direct line with the shore shaft. These were reached at two o'clock, P. M., and the hawsers cut loose. The gates of the crib were opened as soon as it was got in position, and it settled majestically into the lake, where it is ever more to remain, a monument of mind over matter.

When the crib was in place it was filled with stone, with the exception of the center compartment, reserved for the lake shaft to go through, and cables were attached to its corners, which were fastened to the bottom of the lake by means of Mitchell's marine mooring screws, never before used except in tunneling the Thames. The screws had previously been imbedded in the bottom of the lake.

Once in its place, this monster crib became an island in

3

BEECHER'S PATENT IMPROVED
AIR HEATING AND RADIATING FURNACES!
For Anthracite and Bituminous Coal.

A. Crook. B. Heating Chamber. C. Fire Pot. D. Evaporating Pan. E. Feed Door. F. Ash Pit. G. Radiator. H. Air Cylinder. J. Smoke Pipe. K. Cold Air Chamber. L. Radiating Surface.

For Warming Dwellings, Stores, Churches, School Houses, Public Halls, &c.
SIX SIZES, PORTABLE AND BRICK.
Carpenters' Cooking Ranges, Cooking and Parlor Stoves, Refrigerators, Water Filters & Coolers, House Furnishing Goods.

MANUFACTURED AND SOLD BY

F. A. SLACK, 88 La Salle Street,
West Side of the Court House Square,

J. W. FAY would be pleased to see his friends.   **CHICAGO, ILL.**

the lake. When filled with stones it was as immovable as Gibraltar. Reaching down to the clay bottom, the water being about thirty feet deep at this point, several feet of the structure remained above the surface of the lake. As winter approached, the top of the crib was covered by a house, constructed with a cupola, where a light and a fog bell were kept at night to warn the mariner of his position, which the law now requires the city authorities to constantly observe. Tugboats plyed between the crib and the city, carrying out supplies to the workmen and conveying visitors to the wonderful island.

The next end to be obtained was sinking the cylinders in the crib, in order that tunneling could commence in both directions. The winter of '65 was at hand. A large quantity of brick and mortar were taken out and piled upon the crib, as well as provisions for the men; it being anticipated that when winter set in, the ice would not permit of reaching the crib for months at a time.

THE LAKE SHAFT.

The "crib" was now in its place, anchored securely in the lake, two miles from the shore shaft. Every day the workmen in the "bore," or Tunnel proper, were progressing towards it, slowly but surely overcoming the impediments in their way, and gradually becoming more inured to their close and somewhat dangerous quarters.

The huge iron cylinders, which were to form the lake shaft of the Tunnel, were at length got out upon the crib, after much vexatious delay and expense to the contractors. These cylinders are nine feet in diameter, and the iron is two and a half inches thick. They were cast at Pittsburgh, Pa., in nine-feet sections, their immense weight rendering it otherwise impossible to move them. The end of each section was provided with a heavy flange, through which it could be bolted to the one below it, similarly constructed. These cylinders are seven in number, their respective weight being about eleven tons. The irons used in bolting them together were one and a half inch, cemented as well as riveted in their places.

These immense cylinders once placed upon the crib, the next step was to get them in place in the center compartment of the structure. Mr. Bramhall, one of the engineers, solved the problem, inventing machinery and tackle for the occasion. The cylinders were partially suspended over the chasm in the crib by this tackle, then swung upon ways and supports of timber, in which manner they were at last placed in position and firmly riveted together. After reaching the bottom of the lake, on which the crib rested, being sunk into the clay several inches by its immense weight, these cylinders, or sections of the shaft, were sunk into the ground twenty-seven feet, in much the same manner as the shore shaft was built, at which distance they reached the required depth, leaving a fall of two feet to the mile in a straight line drawn to the bottom of the shore shaft.

A complete shaft in the lake was thus formed, by means of the crib. The drawing on the first page shows it fully, and should be closely examined.

The work now resolved itself into simply this: An island (the crib) is situated in Lake Michigan, two miles from shore, upon which (to draw a homely illustration that all will understand) are confined a number of convicts. There is no means of their escape to the city over the surface of the water, and they resolve to go *under it*. Never dreaming of this trick, the authorities have placed in their hands picks and spades, with which to till the island whereon they are confined for life. The villains go to work, dig a hole in the island until its bottom is below the bottom of the lake, then strike off for the shore, which they succeed in reaching after years of toil, much to the surprise of everybody. This is the plan of the Tunnel, the crib forming an artificial island where the water is to enter, and pass to the shore, free from the impurities of the river or the city sewers.

Winter was now rapidly approaching and threatening to lock the lake and river in icy armor. Consequently, every means of getting winter supplies to the crib before the river should freeze up, and stop the running of the tugs, was resorted to. A large supply of brick, cement and other material used in making the Tunnel, was taken out and stored in the building upon the crib. It being anticipated that months might elapse before the miners could communicate with the shore, a commissary department was thought necessary, and all kinds of provisions were likewise transported to the crib, in sufficient quantities to satisfy the hunger of a large number of laborers for some length of time. The services of a cook were also procured, a kitchen commissariat fitted up, and everything put in complete order for the winter campaign under the lake.

A visit to the crib just before the harbor froze over, proved interesting in the extreme. The party was composed of aldermen Denio and Marsh, of Boston, Mr. J. B. Stearns, superintendent of the Boston Fire Alarm Telegraph, and several members of the Board of Public Works, and Chicago citizens. Within this "castle at sea" everything presented the appearance of the interior of a well regulated building on shore, while just without the waves of an angry lake were beating with remorseless fury, but which were not able to even stir the monster artificial island. The steam engine was at work moving heavy stones and timbers into position, workmen were hollowing "heave! ho, heave!" and the dismal creak of powerful pulleys and levers told that a great work was in progress. The Bostonians asked many questions, all of which were carefully answered by Col. Gowan. They expressed many doubts as to the two sections of the Tunnel meeting, but were assured that they would do so to within an inch.

J. M. BRUNSWICK & BRO'S,

BILLIARD TABLE,

MANUFACTURERS,

Importers and Wholesale Dealers in

Billiard Cloths and Balls, French Chalk, Cue Tips, Cue Cement, Plain and Fancy Cues,

AND OTHER MATERIALS BELONGING TO THE TRADE.

Office and Salesroom, No. 72 Randolph Street. Manufactory, Nos. 74, 76 and 78 Randolph Street, Chicago, Ill.

(P. O. Box, 5994.)

Tables supplied with **J. M. Brunswick's** Patent Combination Cushions at short notice.

RAILROADING UNDER LAKE MICHIGAN.

There was something strikingly romantic in the scene, which will never be obliterated from the minds of those present at that time. Fifty workmen living an entire winter in a castle built in the lake, two miles from shore—a little world within a world. The storms and tempests of a large body of water beating around them in every direction, and they busy digging deeper and farther beneath the lake, as if burrowing out of a prison fortress.

The lake shaft being ready, tunneling was commenced from the bottom towards the shore, on the first day of the New Year, 1866. The first brick at the crib end was laid on the 22d day of December, 1865. At that time the shore shaft had reached the length of 4,815 feet. The earth removed from the face of the Tunnel was carried up the shaft and dumped into the lake, and as it progressed similar appliances to the furtherance of the work were used to those already described at the shore shaft.

Leaving the two mining parties under the lake, slowly approaching each other, guided by skillful engineering, we deviate from the bare detail of operations, go back a little, and narrate the particulars of several visits to the shore shaft.

GEN. GRANT'S PARTY VISIT THE TUNNEL.

Early in July, 1865, Gen. Grant and suite arrived in Chicago, and were entertained for several days by the citizens, making the Tremont House their headquarters. Being invited to visit the Tunnel, an hour was fixed upon for their reception at the "big bore," which had then progressed several thousand feet from the shore.

Whenever a person went into the Tunnel, he was obliged to prepare for the work before him. Col. Gowan kept on hand a large variety of tunnel costumes, of the most elegant subterranean designs. He marched the visitors to the clothing room, which consisted of a large chest in his office, and showing them the collection, bade them make choice of their apparel, stipulating that however fascinated they might

become with its fit, and their own figure when attired, they
must on no account wear away a single article, nor take a
shred home with them as a relic of their visit. This being
arranged, the major generals were first given their choice of
garments. Gen. Ord, who is a tall six-footer and rather slim,
picked out a corduroy jacket, which came down as far as his
hips, and there paused. It sat admirably, the sleeves being
a little shorter than his arms, which Col. Gowan assured him
was all the rage, Napoleon having worn a similar coat on a
recent visit to the great Mont Cenis tunnel under the Alps.
Quite Napoleonic looked the general when attired, and he
was cheered for his success in tunnel drapery. Next his
military hat went by the board, and a *chapeau* of a very
slouchy appearance took its place. Rolling up his trowsers he
declared himself ready for a visit to China, or anywhere else.

Gen. Wilcox next fixed up, in a very long coat, being a
moderately short man. This was a .satinet garment, very
threadbare from long aquaintance with the Tunnel, and longer
with the world. The general looked like farmer Slocum just
come to town with a load of vegetables. A palm leaf hat
sat jauntily on his caput, giving him a decided Yankee air.
Gen. Williams borrowed a coat from ·a miner, because he
thought the coat might know more about the Tunnel than any
other, and he would be less likely to go astray from the rest
of the party. A dilapidated tile finished his outfit, and he
stood before the admiring spectators a veritable tunnel
miner.

Superintendent Rice, of the Michigan Central railroad,
got on a very narrow little cap, something on the clerical
style. The coat he wore was once·broadcloth, but that was
before Chicago was a city. When it was cut there was not
a railroad in Illinois; hence the very grotesque appearance
of a railroad man in such a garment.

The remaining members of the party attired themselves in whatever was at hand, some turning their coats inside out and tying handkerchiefs over their heads.

Col. Gowan had prepared three earth cars for the voyage under the lake. These vehicles were about three feet long and two feet wide, and, when used for carrying passengers, were expected to hold four persons. On this occasion they were upholstered with blankets and buffalo robes, and were quite comfortable to travel in.

The cars were brought forward, placed upon the elevator, and four persons got into each one. At last as they were filled they descended into the shaft; the explorers bidding adieu to those behind as their heads went down out of sight. When the cars were lowered to the bottom of the shaft, they were rolled off into the Tunnel proper, as they came down, and coupled to each other, like a railway train, on a genuine track extending the whole length of the bore. When everything was in readiness, or, as Superintendent Rice said, when the train was made up, a diminutive mule was attached, and a miner with a little lamp on his hat drew rein over him, gave a shrill whistle, and the train moved off into the subterranean darkness.

"Now we are under lake Michigan," said Col. Gowan, and the mule was given the whip. Off went the cars at a breakneck speed; into the darkness, into the bowels of mother earth, under the waters of the lake. The rapid motion caused a current of air, which relieved the damp sensations of the place.

After a journey of fifteen minutes, through a straight dark road, at a cantering speed, the train emerged into the last chamber, which was lighted by innumerable little lamps. The miners looked bewildered at the strange advent, and laughed outright as the parties stepped from the cars, and shook themselves. Col. Gowan announced that they had about four hundred feet further to traverse on foot, before they got to the extreme end of the Tunnel. Taking a lamp, he led the way. The long men in the party doubled themselves up and followed, and the short men bent their heads very low.

44

MAMMOTH PAPER COLLAR HOUSE

LARGEST WEST OF NEW YORK.

No. 76 STATE STREET CHICAGO.

GARDEN CITY COLLAR CO.

PAPER COLLARS CUFFS & BOSOMS.

COLLARS WITH STONER'S PATENT BUTTON HOLE

MANUFACTURERS OF AND WHOLESALE DEALERS IN

PLAIN FANCY & ENAMELED ENAMELED GAROTE

LARGEST WEST OF NEW YORK.

"Tramp, tramp, tramp," until backs and legs ached, and at length the extreme end of the Tunnel was reached. About twelve feet was dug into the solid clay, and the miners, who stood about the weird place like so many specters, were engaged in bricklaying and cementing. Colonel Gowan announced that the party were then 3,400 feet from shore, under lake Michigan. Bits of the clay were pocketed as trophies, and the party retraced their steps.

The cars were re-entered at the first chamber, where the party left them, and off went the train in the direction of the shaft, at the rate of 2.40 per mile. The mule, which wore no breeching or back strap, suddenly paused, when the train was at its greatest speed. The cars ran upon the animal's heels, and those in the forward car had the pleasure of receiving him into their laps, nearly frighened out of his mulish wits. Col. Gowan, the conductor of the train, got out, and went ahead to see what had frightened the "locomotive." A shout told the party that some joke was in store for them. He returned to the cars with Senator Chandler's hat, which had been blown off and left on the track during the outward voyage. The mule was not used to such a strange sight, and nearly caused an accident to the passengers.

The party soon emerged into the light of open day, and, congratulating each other on the success of the trip, disrobed and put on their usual habiliments. After shaking hands with and thanking Col. Gowan for his kindness, they got into their carriages and drove back to the Tremont House, well satisfied with their trip into the bowels of the earth, and under lake Michigan.

BOSTONIANS VISIT THE "BIG BORE."

A few weeks after the above excursion, Chicago had the honor of entertaining a delegation of aldermen and other city officials from the "hub." Of course they must see the

Tunnel, and a journey under the lake was put upon the pro
gramme, especially as the guests all requested it, saying
that it was one of the principal things they had come to see.
The party were the same that visited the crib, in a former
chapter.

The first step previous to the descent was examining the
hoisting machinery, and the apparatus by means of which
the air in the Tunnel was kept pure. Everything was fully
explained by Col. Gowan, who took pains to carefully eluci-
date every point and answer every question. The machinery
was beautiful in the extreme, the hoisting machine being
almost noiseless in its revolution, and perfectly under the
control of the engineer. It was so arranged that in case of
an accident it could be stopped in an instant, midway of the
descent. The immense bellows which created a current of
pure air in the Tunnel, was also examined, as a point of
especial interest.

The next thing was to get ready for the descent. Aldermanic broadcloth, fresh and glossy from the looms of Lowell,
could never survive contact with the clay of lake Michigan.
Col. Gowan again drew on his wardrobe, and produced several
complete suits of exploring garments.

"Hoist away," cried the man in charge of the elevator at
the shaft, and the next moment Aldermen Marsh and Denio,
and a miner with a little lamp upon his cap, were rapidly
descending the shaft. Those left on *terra firma* gathered
around the opening in the earth, and gazed after the glim-
mering light as it slowly went down into the bowels of mother
earth; for the lake roared and tossed half a rod away, and
those accompanying the taper were going beneath its waves
and foam. Forsaking the sublime for the ridiculous, a wicked
fellow above remarked that it was an awful lowering of
aldermanic dignity, which provoked a laugh that rang out
clear upon the night air. Luckily for his head the members
of the Boston city government were out of hearing.

Depositing its passengers at the bottom of the shaft, the
elevator was drawn up, and the lesser lights of the party
began the descent. Once upon the bottom of the shaft,

which is eighty-nine feet in depth, the Tunnel proper was seen branching off under the lake like a long tube. In the little chamber where the expectant party was standing, was noticed a train of three small cars, which had been prepared. to convey them out under the lake.

A diminutive mule was attached to this train, and the gentlemen seated themselves like Turks upon their curled-up legs in the bottom of the cars. . One man in each car was given a small lamp, and one was hung upon the mule's collar. The driver's whip was applied vigorously, and away went the train, aldermen and all, under lake Michigan. The Tunnel is five feet in diameter, a perfect cylinder, and just large enough to admit of the passage of the cars. Whoever raised his head above the sideboards would be sure to lose his hat, and a portion of his scalp.

Along the Tunnel ran a pipe, something like a stove pipe, through which the bad air was extracted from the extreme end. As the work progressed, this pipe was extended. The only caution necessary on the railroad excursion under the lake, was to keep one's head clear of the pipe, which all succeeded in doing. Every thousand feet the travelers arrived at a chamber, where the miners mixed their cement and mortar, and where cars were turned around on turn-tables. As you went down into the bore, or further out, the number of feet you had progressed under the lake was marked upon the masonry in plain figures.

The cars could go no further than the last chamber, and the party alighted. Here they found men engaged in mixing mortar and cement, by the light of little lamps hung upon sticks stuck in the clay. Two hundred feet yet remained to be traversed before the extreme end could be reached. The miner who conducted the party led the way with a lamp, and the several gentlemen followed on foot. Men of ordinary

stature were obliged to stoop almost double, so the last part of the journey was where the romance came in. At length the extreme end was reached—nearly a mile from the shaft.

Here all was busy labor. The sharp click of the trowel, and the dull sound of the miner's pick as it was buried into the compact clay, met the ear. The smoke from a dozen fluid lamps floated off into the long, tube-like bore, casting weird shadows over the scene. Clambering over a pile of clay, awaiting transportation to the shaft by the next train, the party reached the miners. Here two stalwart men, with breasts bared and brawny muscles uncovered, were striking herculean blows against the earth before them, which yielded reluctantly, and crumbled. The air here was extremely bad, caused by the number of persons breathing it and the smoke from the lamps. The miners looked like grim specters, as they plied pick and spade and trowel. For a few moments the visitors gazed awe-struck upon the inhabitants of the subterranean world. One miner said that he had been there every day for nearly two years; and so his sallow countenance, and sunken, almost unearthly face indicated.

In the excavating process jets of gas were frequently struck, which delayed the work, and were difficult to surmount. One week several such jets were encountered, and much delay occasioned. The miners could always tell by the sound of their picks when such a jet was being approached. When within a few feet of it they bored through the clay with an auger, and when the jet was reached, one miner pulled the instrument out, and another lit the jet with his lamp. In this manner a natural gas light was produced, sometimes lasting several hours. When the gas was encountered in large quantities it drove the workmen from the Tunnel. To avoid accidents when working new gas jets a safety lantern was used. Few stones were met with. When found at all, they did not seem to lie in any geological order, or range in any particular direction, or strata, but lay in groups of four or five, as if thrown together by the action of the waves at some remote period. When granite was found, it appeared polished, as if having been under the same influence.

The Boston men evinced a desire to lay a brick in the great Chicago Lake Tunnel, thereby immortalizing themselves, and, more particularly, that they might tell of what they had done. So an obliging miner arranged the cement, and the aldermen each deposited a brick, leaving a greenback in the itching palm of the accommodating but greedy workman. Bits of the clay were carefully picked up and pocketed as *souvenirs*, and the tired party of explorers retraced their steps.

Returning to the first chamber, the party re-embarked on the cars, and were soon at the shaft. The elevator placed them upon *terra firma* in a few moments afterwards, all safe and sound. On examining watches, it was found they had spent an hour and a half in the Tunnel.

SIR MORTON PETO AT THE TUNNEL.

When Sir Morton Peto and party visited Chicago, the lake Tunnel was one of the first sights they requested to see. After a drive through the city, these distinguished foreigners were taken to the Water Works, where, unfortunately, they did not find Col. Gowan. The superintendent would not consent to the party entering the cars and going out where the miners were at work, as he stated that an earth train was then about leaving the face of the Tunnel, and the party would be sure to encounter it. He, however, did all in his power to explain the work to the visitors. They were lowered to the bottom of the shaft, each one being provided with a small lamp, to enable him to examine more closely the masonry and note the dimensions of the bore. Sir Morton evinced the greatest interest in the work. Taking a lamp he ran off into the Tunnel until quite beyond the hearing of the remainder of the party, seemingly desirous

of seeing all that was to be seen. He expressed an earnest wish to go to the further end and witness the work in progress, but was told that it was nearly a mile there, and reminded that the "down train" was almost due. The Englishmen took full notes of the work in their diaries, and carried across the Atlantic with them more knowledge of the lake Tunnel than is possessed to this day by half the people of Chicago.

It was intensely gratifying to see these far-sighted Englishmen, with ideas enlarged by the most liberal travel, taking so much interest in the Tunnel. Sir Morton did not hesitate to pronounce it a greater work than the tunneling of the river Thames, yet that required the work of half a century, and was several times entirely abandoned before being brought to completion. It could not even be compared to tunneling under the river at Washington street, for the passage of street cars and other vehicles, now likewise in progress.

SCENES AND INCIDENTS IN THE TUNNEL.

It can easily be imagined that while the miners worked day and night, week after week, month after month, year after year, down in the bowels of the earth, directly under a large and ever restless body of water, that scenes and incidents occurred which would interest the world above ground, could they all be related with any sort of accuracy or coloring that would do them justice.

One of the miners once stated to the writer that none of them were ever entirely without fear. Their situation, the terrible darkness which always surrounded them, the weird shadows of the place, the impossibility of escape should the earth cave or a crevice be opened with the lake, which would instantly submerge them—all these never left their minds. The superstitious were easily able to conjure up all kinds of infernal demons in the narrow passage they left between themselves and the outside world as they advanced, and many

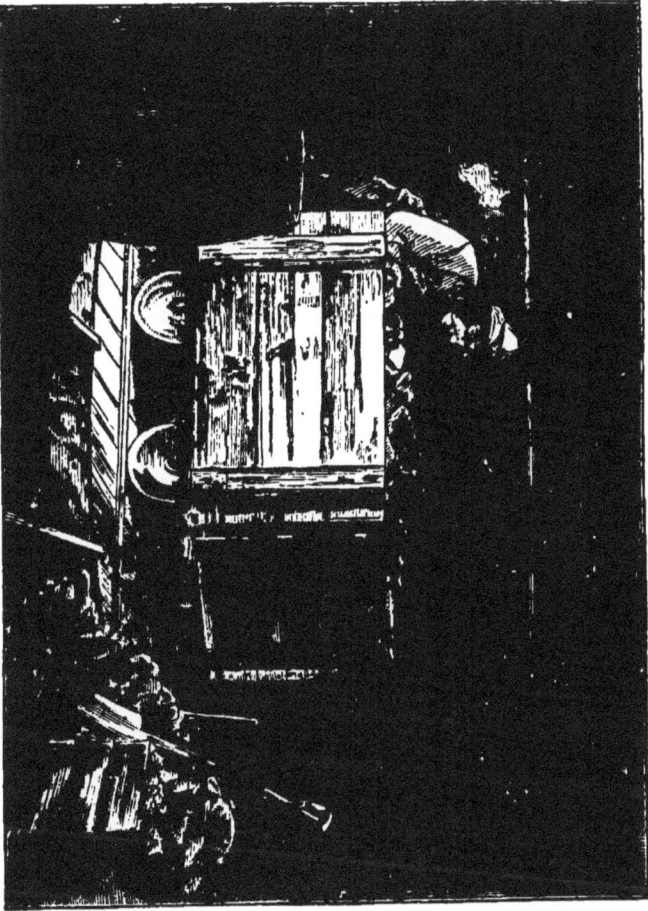

THE TURNTABLE IN THE TUNNEL.

were the times these men fell on their knees to ask for aid
from above, as some unusual sound or occurrence reminded
them of their exact situation, and that they were wholly at
the mercy of the natural influences of the place. In this
sub-lacustrine abode, so full of romance, thought and appre-
hension, where the full power of nature was visible, these
invaders of her solitude cowed before the horrible thoughts
which, in spite of themselves and their work, would arise.
Confine a hardened criminal in such a cell, let him fully
understand that but a wall of clay keeps the waters of the
lake from drowning him, that, should the bellows at the
shore end of the Tunnel cease to perform its rapid revolu-
tions, his lungs would refuse to receive life from the close
and confined atmosphere, and he would repent his sins in an
hour. The horrors of the Inquisition would be weak in
comparison.

Veins of natural gas were frequently encountered by the
miners, which often proved dangerous in the extreme.
Becoming somewhat accustomed to these freaks of nature,
they at length began to treat them uniformly and with
success. The sound of their picks as they struck them into
the clay ahead, on the face of the excavation, told them
when they were approaching a vein. When within a certain
distance of it, they bored into the earth with a sort of auger,
pulling it out the instant the vein was struck, and applying
their lamp. The gas would instantly ignite, burn with
a bright, clear flame, which lit up the Tunnel for a long
distance with a fitful glare. Some of these jets would burn
several hours, obliging the workmen to leave the Tunnel,
and await the extinction of the vein, when they would again
proceed as before.

One day, while Col. Gowan was showing a party of
visitors into the Tunnel, they distinctly heard the paddle

Office & Salesroom, 72 Randolph Street.

J. M. BRUNSWICK & BROS.

Billiard Table Manufacturers.

MANUFACTORY,

Nos. 74, 76 and 78 Randolph Street,

P. O. Box 5994.   **CHICAGO, ILL.**

wheels of a steamer, which just at that moment passed directly over their heads, on the lake, showing that the water and the earth were both good sound conductors. Returning to the outer world, they descried the vessel steaming her way towards the harbor. The workmen frequently reported hearing similar sounds.

In September, 1865, a crevice was struck, through which water began to drip into the Tunnel. The frightened miners fled in dismay, but soon returned, repaired the crevice, and proceeded with their work.

It is somewhat wonderful that during three years of tunneling no accident occurred of any moment, or which delayed the work more than a few days at the furthest. The beds of quicksand, prognosticated by some, were never found.

PECUNIARY DIFFICULTIES.

The history of nearly all great enterprises has been embarrassments in more ways, than one. It has been said that money would remove mountains, which nobody can doubt, since the completion of the lake Tunnel. It was not expected that such a gigantic work could be done for anything less than a mine of gold; neither did anybody suppose that such a job could be accurately figured upon in the office of the Board of Public Works. The great disparity in the bids put in by different parties, which ranged from $239,548 to $1,050,000, is evidence enough of the assertion. The varying state of gold, the prices of labor and material, rendered it still more difficult to tell what the work would cost. The labor market undergoes many changes in three years, which has been the case since the Tunnel was commenced. The contractors also claim that they expected to use the clay for making brick for the masonry, but that it was not fit for the purpose, and they consequently lost a large amount of money.

The contract price of the Tunnel was $315,139, with the allowance of a few insignificant extras. For that amount

the contractors believed they could complete the work, but speedily complained that the compensation was not adequate. According to the contract, it was agreed that monthly estimates of the work would 'be made by the Board of Public Works, during its progress; and that seventy-five per cent. of the amount should be paid to the contractors from time to time; the remaining twenty-five per cent. being retained by the Board until the completion of the work, as security for the faithful performance of the duties of the contractors.

The first application of Messrs. Dull & Gowan was for a simple advance of money; and this request the Council granted, by reducing the amount of monthly estimates reserved by the Board of Public Works from twenty-five to fifteen per cent.

Subsequently, in the fall of 1865, the contractors petitioned for an increase of the contract price, claiming that they took the work when gold was 1.25. When, however, the contract was signed gold was at 1.60; and although it has been higher since, it has also been lower. The price of material has certainly been higher; but, then, it was claimed, on the other side, that the contractors went in with their eyes open, and could have contracted for all the material at the low prices.

The question was referred to the Committee on Finance of the Common Council, who, on the 12th of February last, presented a long and carefully compiled report, amounting to nothing, save the recommendation that the subject be again referred to the Board of Public Works for further investigation. On the 19th of the same month, after a sharp contest in the Council, an ordinance was passed, by a vote of eighteen to eleven, giving to Messrs. Dull & Gowan, in addition to the sum of $315,139 named in the original

contract, the further amount of sixty per cent. on said contract price. This addition amounted to about $189,000. On the 5th of March, this ordinance was returned to the Council without the approval of the Mayor, for the reason that it had not been drawn by the law officer of the city, and was in violation of the charter. The Council then passed an order, advancing the contractors the sum of $50,000, said sum to be deducted from the moneys due said contractors upon the completion of the work.

Up to March 31, 1864, there had been expended upon the work $2,919.63; up to March 31, 1865, $106,389.24; and up to March 31, 1866, $230,220.08—amounting in the aggregate, up to last date, to $339,528.94. Whether or not the contractors have made money out of the job will probably not soon appear, and the matter of further compensation lies between themselves and the city authorities. The press of the city has uniformly argued that no advance should be allowed the contractors, while the Board of Public Works have seemed inclined to concede to their wishes. It is understood that memorandums of the cost of the work have been carefully kept, and a proper adjustment of the matter will no doubt be made. The great question has been, would the Tunnel prove a success? which has been satisfactorily answered.

When completed, the entire expenditure will not be far from six hundred thousand dollars.

THE TUNNEL COMPLETED.

On Saturday, the 24th of November, 1866, the morning papers informed the citizens of Chicago, that the two sections of the Tunnel had progressed so near to each other, that but a thin wall of clay remained to divide them. The glorious result sent a thrill of joy to every heart, and the telegraph carried it to every quarter of the globe. The long anticipated time had arrived—the vexing question as to whether the two mining parties would meet, or, from some

5

slight error of the engineers, pass by each other, and continue on tunneling at random, was answered. When it was further announced that the sections had met each other to within the space of an inch, wonder at the grand result took the place of joy. It was the topic on every tongue, and had the authorities but hinted at a celebration, the city would have resounded with the booming of cannon and ringing of bells: But it was thought best to postpone the grand jubilee until water flowed through the Tunnel, as months of work remained to be done, before the final result would be obtained.

The measurement of the Tunnel, as it then stood, was as follows:

	FEET.
Whole length of Tunnel	10,587
Excavated on Shore Shaft	8,275
Excavated on Lake Shaft	2,290
Remaining	2

Towards evening, the last day of November, the contractors, Messrs. Dull & Gowan, Mr. E. S. Chesbrough, the original "inventor" of the Tunnel, together with his assistant engineer, Mr. Offerman, the superintendent, and a number of miners, dividing themselves into two parties, descended the respective shafts of the Tunnel, for the purpose of removing the thin wall of clay that yet remained between the two sections. The party that descended the shore shaft arrived at the scene of operations first, the others having to traverse two miles of the lake on board a tug, then descend the crib shaft, and go out to meet them. When the appointed time, twenty minutes to four o'clock, arrived, the picks were raised, and soon the barrier was removed, rendering the great lake Tunnel one continuous tube, two miles in length and five feet in diameter, reaching from the shore to the artificial island in the lake.

The greetings of the two parties that thus met under the lake, can be better imagined than described. There were hearty hand shakings, joyful congratulations, and loud huzzas, which resounded through the cavernous depths. Mr. Offerman, superintendent of the work, was the first who stepped from one section to the other of the Tunnel. The joy of the contractors, at this happy termination of their gigantic labor, cannot be described with any sort of justice. But they were not more pleased than were the people of Chicago when they heard the glad tidings. The party that had come down *via* the crib, consisting of Mr. Dull, Mr. Bramhall and others, proceeded westward, and soon arrived at the shore, being the first who passed completely through the Tunnel, from the crib.

On the night in which it was anticipated that the Tunnel would be completed, the gang of workmen were in charge of E. W. Offerman, son of the superintendent. That gentleman had received instructions to pursue the excavation to a certain distance, and then leave it. Twice had he measured and found that he had already permitted the workmen to go forward to the farthest extremity, and yet the rod driven from the other side had not been reached. What was to be done? Had all their calculations been for naught? Was the shaft larger than had been supposed, or had the true course been deviated from? Seizing an auger near at hand, he thrust it into the clay, and commenced boring. A few turns, and it gave way before him as the point was faced upon the other side. The "trimming out" process revealed the iron rod, and the workmen returned to the mouth of the shaft to make the early morning ring with their rejoicing.

The site of the new Water Works is to be the same as the old, with the addition of 187¼ feet of land west of Pine street, which the Board has purchased of Mr. Lill, and upon which, covering both it and the old site, the new building will be erected, the foundations for which are already laid. The erection of this magnificent structure, which will cost, when completed, $55,000, will delay for several months the final letting in of water through the Tunnel. This building should have been erected long before the two sections of the Tunnel met, but the Board considered themselves too much engrossed in that work, to undertake another before it was successfully completed.

A new pumping engine, sufficiently powerful to elevate into the reservoirs, from the Tunnel, eighteen million gallons of water in twenty-four hours, has been purchased, which will be placed in the new building. This engine, which is the largest ever put up in the West, cost $112,350. It was built from designs drawn by Mr. Cregier, the old engineer at the Water Works, and is a model of beautiful machinery.

The last work performed will be to remove the stones which now fill the crib, and lay them in the cement. This will render the structure imperishable, even should the timbers of which it was originally formed decay.

By a glance at the drawing on the first page, the entire plan of the Tunnel will be understood at once. The shore shaft and crib are both shown, the miners are seen at work tunneling from either direction, and the lake, with vessels floating upon its bosom, lies over head.

THE SEALING STONE PUT IN PLACE.

On Thursday morning, December 6th, 1866, people noticed that a large flag floated from the cupola of the Court House, in which building the Board of Public Works have their office. It was in honor of the final closing up of the Tunnel arch, at the point where the crib and shore sections met.

The Board of Public Works had previously extended invitations to the Common Council, Board of Education, and

O. F. FULLER,   E. B. FINCH,   H. W. FULLER,
CHICAGO.   LONDON.   NEW YORK.

FULLER, FINCH & FULLER,

22, 24, 26 & 28

Market St., Chicago

Importers and Wholesale Dealers in

DRUGS, MEDICINES

Paints,
Dye Stuffs,
Chemicals,

WINDOW GLASS, PUTTY,

SOAP MAKERS' STOCK,

TANNERS' STOCK, &c.

Druggists' Sundries,

DIRECT IMPORTATIONS.

Terms Cash. Prices Low. Prompt Shipments.

BRICKING UP THE ARCH.

GENTLEMEN'S
FURNISHING GOODS

J. H. O'BRIEN'S
PERFECT FITTING SHIRTS!

I have now open and ready for inspection, a new and complete Stock of

FINE FURNISHING GOODS

Adapted for the season, consisting in part of the following:

Full Lines of Hosiery and Gloves.
Silk Scarfs, new and novel styles.
Silk Ties, both black and fancy.
Linen-Cambric Handkerchiefs, hemstitched and fancy.
Merino Wrappers and Drawers.
English Braces.
F. and C. Red Wrappers and Drawers.
French and American Suspenders.
Lamb's Wool Wrappers and Drawers.
A Full Line of Linen and Paper Collars.
Golden Flax Shirts, a complete assortment.
Linen, Muslin and Jean Drawers.
Plain and Fancy Traveling Shirts, &c., &c.

TO ALL OF WHICH I INVITE YOUR ATTENTION.

JOHN H. O'BRIEN,
88 DEARBORN ST., CHICAGO,

Send for a Circular.   Opposite the Masonic Temple.

many other prominent citizens, to witness the ceremonies. At the time fixed, about two hundred of the invited guests were on the spot, awaiting anxiously the rare adventure before them.

The Board of Public Works had arranged to have two trains of cars pass through the Tunnel, from the shore to the crib, one leaving the shore shaft at ten o'clock and the other at half-past twelve, in the morning; and also to have a tugboat leave State street bridge, at corresponding hours, for the crib. Those who went out by the Tunnel railway were to return via the lake, and those who reached the crib by means of the tugboats, were to return to the shore through the Tunnel, on board the train which brought the other party. Twenty-one earth cars were put in readiness for the Tunnel trip, and the tugboat S. H. Crawford was chartered for service above the waves. The hour for starting was ten o'clock, at which time the entire party were on hand, full of eager expectation.

When the hour arrived, His Honor, Mayor Rice, the several members of the Board of Public Works, the Common Council, and as many of the other guests as could ride in the first train, were lowered into the shore shaft, where they entered the cars. The Mayor took the first car, to reach which he was obliged to do considerable crawling upon his hands and knees, and the other members of the party arranged themselves in the train, four persons occupying a car, one sitting in each corner. As the memorial stone was to be inserted upon the south side, the passengers were seated so as to face that point of the compass. As described before, the motive power of the train was a mule, which could be dimly discerned in the gloom ahead. When all was in order, the train started off through the tube-like passage, the mule cantering along at a rapid pace. Many were the jests and jokes indulged in on this wonderful highway, as the cars sped out under the lake. There was also considerable temerity exhibited, as some of the passengers had never before visited the Tunnel.

At the distance of a mile and a half from shore, at the

GREAT SALE

—OF—

MEN'S AND BOYS'

READY-MADE

CLOTHING,

—TO—

CLOSE THE PARTNERSHIP

—OF—

G. T. BELDING & CO.

THIS

MAMMOTH STOCK

WILL BE

OFFERED TO THE PUBLIC

AT A

GREAT SACRIFICE!

BELDING & CO.

98, 100 & 102 Randolph Street, Chicago.

exact point where the two tunneling parties met, the train stopped. The Mayor and Board of Public Works left their seats, and advanced to the spot. Mr. Kershall, the City Inspector, said:

Mr. Mayor, and Members of the Common Council:

You have arrived at the spot where the two ends of the work are to be closed up. It only remains for you, Mr. Mayor, to place the last stone in position in this work, and we are going to help you do it.

Mayor Rice then came forward, and spoke as follows, amid the cheers of the guests:

Members of the Board of Public Works, of the Board of Aldermen, Gentlemen Contractors and Fellow Citizens:

At the commencement of this important work, the Mayor of the city, being its chief officer, and supposed to represent the sentiments of all our citizens, was appointed to remove the first shovelful of earth, thereby introducing that work and showing the world that that great undertaking should be done.

Now that this portion of it is completed, I have the great pleasure, and the honor, as being Mayor of the city, in like capacity to put the last finishing stroke upon this work, which is intended, as I understand it, to show to the world that the citizens of Chicago, through me, give this great work their approval.

His Honor then took the trowel and the stone, a perfectly white block of marble, one foot long by six inches wide, placed the cement in the interstices left in the arch, and finally deposited the key stone in its final place, remarking further as he did so: "Now, gentlemen, in behalf of the city of Chicago, I place the last stone in this great Tunnel —the wonder of America and the world." A number of pieces of American coin were then deposited inside the stone, by the guests, when the Mayor continued: "Gentlemen, I announce to you all, that the last stone in the Tunnel is laid, and that the work is completed."

It was now eleven o'clock, and the party, re-entering the

cars, were soon at the crib shaft, appearing somewhat blinded by the light, as they ascended from beneath the lake. The party who came by the tug were already there, and many were the congratulations exchanged. In a short time the second train from the shore arrived, and the wondering passengers were also elevated to the large room in the crib. At this juncture cannon boomed upon the air, fired simultaneously from the crib and the shore.

After partaking of a fine collation, prepared in the kitchen of the crib, the party that came by the tug started off for the shore, *via* the Tunnel railroad, and the mayor, aldermen, etc., took passage on the tug.

The stone laid by Mayor Rice bore the following inscription:

> **CLOSED,**
> **December 6, 1866.**

www.ingramcontent.com/pod-product-compliance
Lightning Source LLC
Chambersburg PA
CBHW021521270326
41930CB00008B/1038